Advanced
Do-It-Yourself
Brain Surgery

Advanced
Do-It-Yourself
Brain Surgery
and other Big Jobs

Stewart Cowley

a Charles Herridge book
published by

Muller, Blond & White

First published in Great Britain
in 1985 by Muller, Blond & White Ltd
55-57 Great Ormond Street
London WC1N 3HZ

© Copyright Charles Herridge Ltd 1985
Designed by Bruce Aiken
Illustrations by Robin Wiggins
Produced by Charles Herridge Ltd
Woodacott, Northam, Devon EX39 1NB

ISBN 0 584 40009 8

Printed in England

Contents

Dear Reader

Have you ever looked at your life and wondered why you had been given one? Or looked at someone else and wondered why you were never given theirs? Or never looked at anything at all and wondered why you keep falling down open manholes? Well here is your chance to do something about it. Take a deep breath, steel your resolve and change it RIGHT NOW!

Well, okay, so it doesn't always work first time. That is why this book could prove to be a major turning point in your life, a doorway to a brand-new, fulfilling and enriching way of life. At least, it could if it was a much better book. As it is it will have to suffice as a collection of well-meaning hints as to what new career or interest might suit you best.

To extract the most benefit from the possibilities outlined here you must first know yourself, then apologise and promise not to do it again in company. You must *really* want to change. Not just a little, but as much as everybody else wants you to change. Let your enthusiasm for change carry you away. As much as everybody else wants you to be carried away.

Start by getting a piece of paper and a pencil and listing all the good qualities you think you possess. Write really big so you don't waste the paper, then show it to an intimate friend who knows you better than you know yourself to see if it is a realistic self-assessment. Now show it around at a party and get even more laughs.

When you can finally bring yourself to come out of your room, waste no time in throwing yourself into the task of getting stuck into your chosen change of direction, or under a bus if you still can't think of anything to do. The secret is commitment, and if you follow the suggestions in this book as closely as is humanly possible, I have absolutely no doubt that you will be committed.

But make no mistake. The fame and fortune that you will possibly achieve as a result will bring their own difficulties and dilemmas. You will lose some friends but the ones that are really worth having will stick by you as long as you keep throwing money at them. Despite all the excitement and glamour, they are the ones who will stay with you through thick and thin, ethpecially the thinful parts.

You will have to learn entirely new skills such as how to talk on television without spitting, the correct way to address Royalty, and how to get comfortable on the shiny leather seats of the House of Lords without making those noises much favoured by large, elderly dogs.

But despite these demands and stresses, I am certain that you will gain enormous satisfaction from being right in the forefront of your fellow human beings, even if it's only because they are all running in the opposite direction.

S. Cowley

ℬrain ℱurgery

Some Exciting New Ops

The basic techniques for brain surgery are quite good fun but after a few simple operations the thrill wears off. At least that is the case if you are the one doing the operating. After all there's little more to it than making a hole in someone's head and poking about with a torch. Even trepanning becomes boring after a while. However spectacular it may once have been to whip off the top of a guest's head at a party, you will gradually, if not suddenly, find yourself less in demand as a fun person.

Actually, brain surgery is more than a party piece so these early attempts will stand you in good stead should you decide to take things a bit further. Dexterity and experience are important if you wish to tackle more adventurous projects and you ought to try some incredibly difficult techniques.

Unless you have a gift for working with mirrors and a very high pain threshold, you will need subjects to assist your studies. In some respects it is useful having a single subject willing to undergo several ops rather than cluttering your house up with lots of people having just one each. You will save time if you can fit your colleague with a sort of miniature cat-flap. A more sophisticated and certainly less draughty solution is to cut a screw thread around the edge of a circular portion of skull. A small brass or pine cupboard knob can be obtained from most good hardware stores and screwed into the centre to facilitate removal when required. If you are not sure that your home handicraft is up to this, an old sink drain plug will do the trick.

If you are not fortunate enough to have such a co-operative

Alternative methods of providing permanent easy access to the brain.

Brains look very like cauliflowers so always label them after removal, especially if you've just been to the greengrocer's.

friend, try advertising in your local paper. DO NOT just go into the park and start hitting people on the top of the head with a mallet. This is exhausting and time-consuming. Invite them home first. You should also bear in mind that it is a legal requirement to obtain the patient's signature on a consent form before starting to operate. In my own experience I find that the best time for this is after the anaesthetic has been administered. With a credit card or driving licence as reference, use elastic bands to fix the pen firmly in the patient's fingers, grasp the wrist and write clearly and neatly.

Some Incredibly Difficult Techniques

The 180° Turn

Turning the brain completely around inside the skull is definitely incredibly difficult. It is

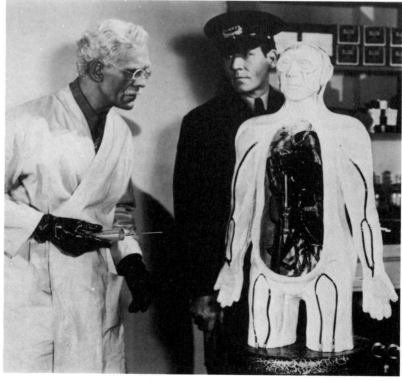

Bionic implant surgery at its best. This torso has been completely stripped out and refitted with a perfect baritone voice and digital alarm. The inventor prepares to start it up.

also somewhat pointless, but good practice for later. Do not try to turn it through more than 360 degrees. If you get over confident and keep going round, the spinal cord will wind up and your patient's legs will spin rapidly. Don't try to get round this problem by strapping their legs down as the spinal chord is likely to twist into those lumpy knots like you get on model aircraft and they will concertina your patient into a dwarf very suddenly. Turning the brain through less of a circle, say 180 degrees, will necessitate making two small holes at the rear of the skull to enable your patient to see out once the operation is over.

Brain Removal

Removing the brain altogether is also fairly tricky. The human brain is actually only one part of the central nervous system and should be removed with all its component parts intact. Make sure that your hands are clean and dry. Brains are notoriously slippery and it is a good idea to place absorbent kitchen towel over it before grasping it firmly and pulling in a single, continuous movement. If all goes well, the brain should come free with the spinal cord and all the peripheral nerves in one piece. If you think that this is a bit tricky, wait until you start trying to put it back. A useful tip here is to use knitting needles to poke the nerves into position.

Do not feel tempted to skip this stage because it is very bad form to wander off and leave someone completely empty. If the worst comes to the worst and you damage or hopelessly tangle the network of nerves you will just have to pack the spaces with crumpled up newspaper and make up the spare bed. Anyway, a spare brain is always useful as a source of parts for other operations you may perform, and will last for quite a long time in the fridge. They look very like

Hitting unsuspecting citizens on the head so that you can operate on them before they begin arguing isn't really a good idea. For a start some people are very heavy and difficult to carry home.

cauliflowers so I should keep it in a separate box and write BRAIN on it. If you or one of your friends are a bit of a whiz with electronics you could wire it up to an electric typewriter and have yourself a very inexpensive home computer.

Cosmetic Brain Surgery

Actually, brains are not terribly attractive parts of the human body so there is plenty of scope for improvement. Yet the number of practitioners of cosmetic brain surgery is very, very small. In fact there aren't any at all, so here is an ideal opportunity to get in on the ground floor of what could easily become a highly lucrative sideline. Because this is such a new field it is not easy deciding where to start, but California would seem to as good a place as any.

With a little thought you could bring a whole new approach to the concept of inner beauty and have film stars falling over

Top secret plan of a bionic saluting device perfected by army scientists and now undergoing field tests under extreme conditions in Finland and the Saraha.

themselves to employ your services. The most obvious problem to tackle is that of wrinkles. Even those blessed with perfect skin have brains that are a mass of unsightly wrinkles, creases and folds. In order to deal with these effectively you should remove as much of the skull as possible to give you plenty of elbow room. Ideally you ought to remove the entire skull as this has the added advantage of avoiding the need to shave portions of the head. Just cut round from the corners of the mouth to the nape of the neck and ease the skull upwards.

The quickest and simplest way of getting rid of brain wrinkles is to make a small incision in the base of the brain close to the Medulla Oblongata. A bicycle pump can then be inserted into the Corpus Callosum and the entire organ inflated until the wrinkles pop out leaving the surface beautifully taut and smooth.

The main drawback of this method is the difficulty in replacing the skull. A liberal application of olive oil or washing up liquid will help considerably, but do not risk bursting the brain by forcing too hard. In such a case you should release some of the air, but this should be done with great care to avoid the possibility of your client flying round and round the room making rude noises.

If your client is unwilling to accept even the few shallow wrinkles left in this instance you may have to remove the hair from the skull and transplant it directly into the brain's surface. Ears can be transferred in the same way and a heavy application of make-up should put matters right.

A slower but less problematic method is to grout the folds and fissures with a spatula and plastic filler. Using gentle strokes you can then apply moisturizer, foundation, powder and blusher in that order for a really beautiful brain that looks young and feels young.

Once you have become a real dab hand at brain surgery, you could tackle really big jobs like brain transplants. Start with something fairly easy like mice or beetles just to get the hang of it, then have a go with some of your friends. Just think what fun you can have after a dinner party by swopping the brains of your guests. Especially if you choose opposite sexes. How you'll all laugh at their confusion when they decide to use the bathroom!

If you feel like expanding your skills you might like to consider bionics. Again this is a field at quite an early stage of development, so you can break fresh ground. Use your experience as a brain surgeon to build some really intriguing people. A Junior Constructors Set, household items, and of course that brain in the fridge you've been wondering what to do with, can all provide the basis for making a new friend.

Skin will be something of a problem, of course, but a lot can be done with papier mâché and paint.

Complete familiarity with human brains can lead to even more delicate projects such as working on miniature brains, like those in household pets. Selective surgery could help our little friends in such areas as personal hygiene, training, overcoming neuroses or depression. But DO NOT attempt such delicate work until you are absolutely sure that you have learned everything necessary from working on larger brains.

This is a particularly interesting operation, being performed by Dr Ludwig Bonkers of Wiesbaden. It involves drilling into one ear and and out of the other, thus enabling the subject not to listen to anyone boring, or to anything else for that matter.

NEIGHBOURHOOD RADIO
your big opportunity

The truth of the matter is that unless you're a real media personality these days, you're nobody at all. The mass communicators are the new aristocracy and they guard their status very jealously, which makes it hard for a newcomer to break into the business. But things are changing rapidly, and if you fancy earning vast sums of loot by chattering away to people you don't know and can't even see about things they're not really interested in, now is a good time to get started.

There's no doubt that being a household name is great fun and will get your name mentioned in many a household. Quite apart from the fact that others will pay you wads of cash just to say the things that ordinary people say for free, you get to watch shoppers poke each other with their elbows every time you pop into the shop for a paper, enjoy hundreds of drinks bought by total strangers and receive thousands of letters that aren't bills.

In the early days of local radio almost anyone could become a media personality and most of them did, but even that is hard to do these days. The answer lies in the newer field of **neighbourhood radio**. The real advantage of the electronic age is that hugely complicated boxes of wires, chips and transistors are extremely cheap, and this makes setting up your own radio or television station both simple and inexpensive.

Radio is the best place to start as it involves the minimum equipment. In fact, all you need to start broadcasting in your own neighbourhood is a large piece of cardboard rolled into a cone through which you can shout or sing out of the bedroom window. Then, once you have gained valuable experience as a media presenter, you can move on to electric radio.

You ought to know a little about this mysterious stuff to set up a proper radio station. It is colourless and odourless and lurks in little secret places ready to jump out and bite you

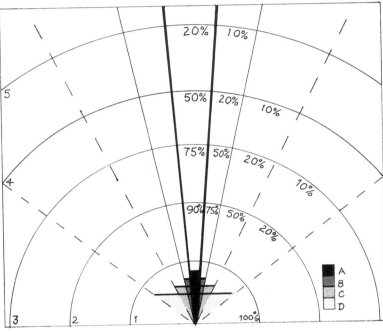

when you least expect it. Even when you do expect it, it can give you a nasty shock. It is kept in long wires or small boxes called batteries, although the latter can only be used to store weak electricity.

As anyone who has stuck their tongue into a mains socket will tell you, the more powerful the current, the more noise it produces. But electric broadcasting is not as simple as putting your cardboard cone to your mouth and grasping the live end of a mains lead, because although you will produce a lot of volume, particularly in the higher frequencies,

To find out how far your megaphone will broadcast, study this diagram. Distance, volume and spread are measurable in direct relationship to the diameter of the megaphone, e.g.

$$\frac{bell}{A} \times 3 = 75\%. \text{ Got it?}$$

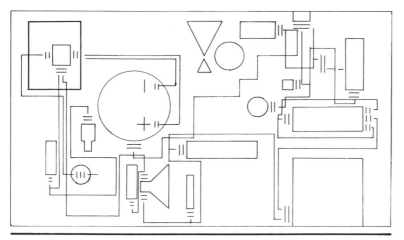

Wiring diagram (above) and illustration (below) of the sort of broadcasting equipment available in any ordinary household. This outfit gives high noise boost without flutter.

no-one will understand much of what you're saying. You could also leave shoe-shaped scorch marks on the carpet.

Instead you will need a microphone, a transmitter and some big aerials. Most components can be salvaged from old TV sets, electric razors, hair driers and washing machines. In fact anything that looks really complicated and has plenty of wires and switches will do. Tape or glue them all together. Follow the wiring diagram illustrated if you're not sure what to do. Then plug it in and switch on.

It will probably take an hour or so for the flames to die down and this is a good opportunity to give some thought as to exactly what you're going to broadcast. Programming is a vital aspect of radio and television and usually consists of planning really cheap and boring programmes for when people are stuck at home, and exciting, lavish productions when they are thinking of going out.

A good mix of shows is the key and some basic categories are outlined below:

Current Affairs

Back to electricity again, only by now you will have learned enough to talk entertainingly about watts, volts and chromosomes to your listeners. One trick of the trade is to talk without a break to make it hard for a listener to turn off in case you slip up and say something interesting. Should you actually forget what you're talking about just start immediately talking about what you're doing or thinking. Unless, of course, it's rude.

Music (serious)

Broadcasting recorded music is too expensive because you have to pay royalties, so live performances are a good idea. Opera is easy because you need only follow the rules for current affairs but as you talk, let your voice go very high and very low, and hum between words. Orchestral works are more difficult unless you play the recorder.

Music (popular)

Forget it. Do-it-yourself popular music is NOT popular.

This looks like a good chat show doesn't it. Everybody calm and relaxed and chatting happily away, probably about swine fever or the price of drinks in Spain. It doesn't really matter as long as they keep talking.

You will find that not everyone wants to be interviewed especially if you're got up a bit strange. In these circumstances it's best to make your excuses and leave.

Chat Shows

Ideal for audience involvement, this. The advantage of starting your career in radio is that you can get amazing celebrities to astonish your neighbours and get them rushing to their windows and peering over your hedge in an exhilarating foretaste of the household namery to come. Provided you can do the voices okay, that is. Don't make silly mistakes and conduct topical and stimulating interviews with someone who has long since passed away. Read obituaries with care. Unless, of course, it's a religious programme, in which case it could do miracles for your ratings.

What you talk about is as important as who you talk to. Even the presence of Omar Sharif will fail to hold a large audience if you insist on discussing the significance of Newtonian Law in supra-orbital physics.

Drama

There's no need to worry too much about scripting this as your programmes will contain more than enough drama if you've wired up your radio station as we have suggested.

If you haven't got a home you can always broadcast from the tops of trees, though our friend here seems to have forgotten that you need an audience. Also he has no megaphone. Silly fellow!

William and Henrietta Ponsonby of Radio Belgravia pose before their prizewinning entry at the 1985 Custom Console Show. You don't really need to go this far but dials are fun, aren't they.

Phone-ins

Audience participation is always a good thing and people love to think that they are eavesdropping on someone else's conversation. If no-one calls in you could route your domestic phone circuit through the transmitter and broadcast all your personal calls.

You will certainly receive some loony phone calls and these are quite good for your ratings. Particularly if you ask them in for an interview, as nothing boosts audience figures as much as the sound of someone going utterly beserk with an axe in a confined space.

Bureaucracy is everywhere! One of the things you'll have to put up with is the Government Inspector of Neighbourhood Radio breathing down your neck and waiting to pounce the minute you say a word like 'bottom'. It's easy to be put off by this, as this picture of Ted Stokes of Radio Free Nether Wallop, looking a bit edgy, shows.

In the right place and at the right time advertising can make a really big impact.

Advertising

There is a lot of money to be made in this area, especially if there are any people listening to your station. If your programmes contain a lot of appalling language and gratuitous sex and violence, many of the major manufacturers will pay you a fortune not to mention their products. Apart from advertising, you can earn a lot through personal appearances at banks, post offices, jeweller's shops and so on. Especially if you're carrying a gun.

Television

Don't pick your nose in front of the camera, it interferes with your diction.

Ghostbursting and How To Do It

(SORT OF)

Box office receipts aside, ghosts are not a good thing. They will often depress people, household pets and property prices, and increase your dry-cleaning bills by suddenly leaping out with bloodcurdling shrieks when you're deep in thought. The problem of dealing with ghosts is complicated by the fact that the modern ghost has come a long way since the good old white sheet and rattling chains days. Most self-respecting spectres, poltergeists or demonic presences have kept well abreast of the times. They are more likely to haunt refrigerators and central heating systems than dingy family seats that have seen better days.

They are also, it seems, a much more aggressive breed than of old and are much more interested in possessing people or expensive household appliances than just wandering about at night, wringing their hands and breathing heavily. This change in attitude on the part of the denizens of the twilight realm has made coping with them something of a problem. The apparent decline in their moral values has made traditional forms of exorcism less effective and has created the need for an entirely new approach to the matter.

Here, then, is an ideal chance for the aspiring exorcist or ghostburster to revolutionize the industry's image and bring modern techniques and technology to this ancient problem. The task is not made easier by the bewildering number of different varieties of supernatural manifestation that exist.

One of the first obstacles to overcome is convincing people that they have need of your services in the first place. It is amazing how often people fail to notice that they are the victims of a sinister presence and blithely go about their daily business without having the slightest idea of the mortal danger they are in. The first duty of the professional ghostburster is to enlighten them.

The best way to start is to look through the local telephone directory. Now and then a name will catch your attention and this is a good sign that the premises are haunted, particularly if business is slow. To confirm your suspicions you should call round and inform the occupants of the danger they are in. If they laugh, jeer, get angry or set the dog on you, you can be certain that the

supernatural resident is trying its best to put you off. In the latter instance the unfortunate animal itself is probably the host in which the demon resides.

Stage two is to let the ghost know that you mean business, and this will involve tackling it on its own terms. In the case of simple spectres, ghosts

The great Edwardian ghostbuster Lawrence de Courtenay (left) allowed his personal collection to pose for the camera in this rare 1914 shot. There are actually 13 ghosts in this picture but 8 have failed to materialize and 2 are in ectoplasmic suspension.

Most night schools offer short courses in self defence. Instructor Bert Vulpine, reformed werewolf and scout leader, demonstrates the werewolf assault with his attractive assistant.

Basic ghostbursting techniques: (v) howling down the chimney to let the ghost know you're there.
(w) swinging past windows in a cellophane dry cleaning wrapper (x) pouring tomato juice in the water tank (y) pumping air into the central heating system to make it knock and bang. After this treatment the ghost is sure to know you're gunning for it.

or phantasms it will mean a few uncomfortable nights perched on the roof, moaning forlornly down the chimney and swinging past bedroom windows on a rope, dressed in those cellophane wrappers that dry-cleaners protect suits with.

With invisible spirits like poltergeists and some demons, you will need to vary your technique. Remove the tiles from a portion of the roof to allow access to the roof space. A few gallons of tomato juice in the water tank will show the occupying demon that he's not the only one who can make the taps run blood. With a bit of skill you could also introduce airlocks into the central heating system which will cause some disturbing

knocks and rattles. For maximum effect, tread between the attic joists.

The third stage begins when your prospective clients recognize the need for your services after all, and the main exorcism can get under way. Your equipment will vary from case to case, but a useful basic kit should include a garden sprayer filled with crushed garlic juice, wolfbane aerosols, a turbocharged vacuum cleaner, a portable pentagram and a family-size thermos flask for keeping ghosts in. A large galvanized dustbin with a small view slit is useful for dealing with any large dogs who have been possessed.

Fear is one of the most potent weapons in the armoury of a demon or phantom and you must learn to overcome it. Learn to whistle without delay as it could mean the difference between sanity and madness. Memorize a few jaunty airs such as 'Old Macdonald's Farm', 'Colonel Bogie' or Wagner's 'The Ring'. If you are able to faithfully reproduce these melodies you may retain your

sanity. If you are unable to carry a melody and can only produce an infuriating drone you will drive others to madness. In this case just laugh a lot as loud as you can.

On entering the haunted structure, don your gas mask and liberally spray all surfaces with the garlic juice until you have the ghost backed into a corner. If it is a poltergeist it will probably start throwing crockery so retire to your dustbin with the nozzle of your vacuum cleaner protruding from beneath the lid and switch on. As soon as you hear the ghost enter the bag, remove it, pour it into the thermos flask and screw on the top.

Do not concern yourself with the fact that most of the china, pictures, small objets d'art and soft furnishings will also find their way into the vacuum cleaner as the noise will make your clients realize the desperate nature of the struggle that is taking place.

This technique should prove adequate for most of the hauntings you are likely to encounter but other forms of supernatural manifestation may require a different approach. The vacuum cleaner

Police artist Doris Schwartzkopf captured this famous moment in 1967. Vampire victim Hilda Brubaker is about to uncover high-society vampire Count Alucard (far right).

method is little use against **zombies**, for example, as even if you succeed in capturing him or her, they will not fit into your thermos flask. They are members of the living dead and cannot therefore be killed. Even if you dismember them the various bits of anatomy will continue to be a nuisance and you could find yourself surrounded by a single person.

The only effective method is to chop them up into bite-sized portions as swiftly as you can and stuff them into a liquidizer. Even though they still will not actually be dead they will cease to be a threat as no-one has actually been torn to shreds by soup, however malevolent.

Vampires are also tricky to dispose of. They are harder to detect than zombies because they are usually in much better physical condition. Vampires can be destroyed by running water, direct sunlight or a stake driven through the heart. By and large the first two methods are the safest to use in case you do make a mistake in identifying a vampire. You are more likely to be forgiven for hosing someone down with a soda siphon than nailing them to the sofa with a fencepost. If you always wear a necklace of garlic cloves you will never be pestered by a vampire. Or anyone else for that matter.

Werewolves also look like ordinary people until they start chasing cars and biting the hubcaps. Another giveaway is the manner in

which werewolves greet each other. Although acutely embarrassing for other passers-by, it is a vital clue for the professional ghostburster.

When werewolves get down to greet each other like this all hell can break loose. To effect your escape, throw a short stick or tennis ball as far as you can, shout 'Fetch' and run as fast as you can (in the other direction).

How To Be a Mercenary
and Not Get Hurt

Although you don't have to be a mercenary to like money, you do have to like money quite a lot to be a mercenary. It's a rough, tough business and the rewards are often high, but cash is not its only merit. It is also a healthy, outdoor way of death that offers the opportunity for plenty of swaggering about and being sick in pubs without having to clean it up.

There are some physical requirements that have to be met so it's no use considering the job of soldier of fortune if you're an utter wimp. However, you can improve your chances quite a lot by adopting a suitable diet and changing your personal habits. You are what you eat so your daily menu should include some rough and rugged foods like suet, spinach sandwiches and pig's trotters. Five thousand calories a day and plenty of exercise should bulk you up to fill out a uniform well.

But more than anything else, your attitude will determine your suitability as a freelance warrior. You must think aggressively if you have to think at all, and be prepared to get cross at the drop of a hat, even if it's someone else's. It's good practice to lose your temper at the slightest thing, but make sure that it's not something that someone else is responsible for as this can lead to unpleasant confrontations. The weather is a good place to start, for example, and puddles can drive you into an apoplectic fury without fear of upsetting anybody.

One of the things you just can't do as a mercenary is burst into tears when the going gets tough. Nobody will take you seriously if you do, not even the enemy.

Getting into a sack to swing through windows and zap terrorists saves you getting cut – and if they haven't seen you getting into it they don't know you're inside, Brilliant!

If there is a shortage of external targets for your rage getting angry with yourself will do. Beating yourself senseless because you don't like the colour of your tie or the way that you're looking at yourself in a mirror is a reasonable substitute. It doesn't matter how often you do this as a little brain damage can stand you in very good stead. Don't go too far though. Shooting yourself in the head will not help your career.

Your general manner should become more manly and will involve things like eating chickens whole with your bare hands and chewing with your mouth wide open. This latter technique is not suitable for drink unless you hate the taste of it. Blowing your nose without a hanky and being sick without bending over are also the hallmarks of virile masculinity.

Even putting aside for a moment deliberate attempts to maim you, some of the physical tasks that you may be expected to undertake can also be pretty hair-raising. One very popular mercenary-type thing is swinging in through other people's top floor windows on the end of a rope. Now broken glass is definitely dangerous stuff and can cause enough bad cuts to let you leak to death.

If you find yourself trapped in a situation like this, the only safe way of doing it is to get inside a heavy canvas bag and tie that to the rope before letting yourself hurtle through the glass. This technique has a further advantage should there be unfriendly people waiting inside with guns or pointed sticks. In such an eventuality, lie very, very still and they might not realize that you are a mercenary at all. In fact, it is very likely that they'll think that somebody else is throwing bags of rubbish through their windows and get cross at passers-by in the street below instead of taking it out on you. If they do happen to look inside the bag you should pretend to be fast asleep.

There are many other skills to learn such as jumping out of loud helicopters, where the trick is to wait until it has landed. The art of camouflage is also very important. It's no use tying huge branches and bunches of grass to your hat if you are in the middle of the desert. Instead of remaining inconspicuous, you are likely to get trampled to death by thirst-crazed legionnaires mistaking you for an oasis. Choose your method of concealment to suit the environment. In the desert cover yourself with honey and roll in the sand. In snowy regions build a hollow cotton-wool snowman. In urban areas wear bricks or an old door.

The life of a mercenary is a changing one; changing uniforms, changing magazines, changing sides, but exciting none the less. You will have plenty of opportunity to travel, often as fast as your legs will carry you, and this brings us to another problem area. Foreign places are often not at all like home and it can be quite hard looking after yourself properly.

Gippy Tummy

The water, for example, is often very bad for you and will give unpleasant, often virulent, tummy upsets. This will have an adverse effect on your role as a brutal mercenary as it is unbelieveably difficult being very butch in rubber underwear. On the other hand it can make enemy troops extremely reluctant to capture you.

One tour of duty is enough for most people, then they can return home and concentrate on the much more rewarding business of being an unemployed mercenary and stand around looking really sinister at parties or showing young girls where you got a nasty splinter from a captured ammunition case.

Camouflage is an art you should study, but remember that what works in one place won't necessarily work in another. That's why combat dress is usually a bit drab.

One of the advantages of being a mercenary is that you don't always have to wear what you're told to. There's equal merit in the traditional (left), futuristic (centre), and ancient (right) styles. Perhaps one of each would be a good idea.

Uniforms

Once you have mastered these techniques you can begin thinking about your uniform and equipment. Mercenaries do not like too much publicity so your single most important item is the balaclava helmet. You can get a suitable pattern from most good haberdasheries that will be well within the capabilities of even the most inexperienced knitter. Dark coloured wools are much the best as pinks and mauves tend to show up in searchlight beams. The more of your face that they cover the better, but it is a mistake to leave out the eyeholes entirely as your colleagues won't

be able to tell if you're awake or dead and might leave you behind.

The rest of your uniform should be made from suitable camouflage material. Don't skimp on this and try and run something up yourself. It's terribly difficult to melt into the shadows dressed in some little number you've thrown together from a red and white checked tablecloth. It should also be very loose-fitting to give you unrestricted freedom of movement. In fact it's not a bad idea if you can turn completely round inside your battledress so that when things are hotting up you can charge *away* from the enemy lines without arousing the suspicions of your colleagues.

On the Job

This brings us to a vitally important point that may well have escaped your attention in the excitement of contemplating your new career. Being a mercenary is actually rather dangerous if you do it properly. Unless you limit yourself to taking local jobs like hit-and-run playground monitor or lollipop man there is a distinct possibility that someone might start shooting bullets at you or making you eat really awful foreign food. Then, as if all the horrors of war are not enough, you may well have to get all sorts of horrid vaccinations.

HEY PRESTO

A PARTICLE ACCELERATOR

We are always hearing about the importance of the nuclear family, but how many of your friends have actually taken the plunge and involved themselves in this fascinating science? Despite the fact that we are all supposed to be living in the Nuclear Age, you will hardly ever hear anyone chatting about fast-breeders, fusion versus fission or radioactive decay rates while standing in the supermarket check-out queue or waiting for a bus!

Why not take the lead in your community and get all the family involved in today's technology? Every man and his dog has got a home computer these days so an ideal way of getting one jump ahead of your fellows is to build yourself a real particle accelerator. It needn't cost a vast amount and could be a stepping stone to much bigger things.

Not that a particle accelerator is that small itself. It will certainly take up much of your home and garden, but will surely make you the envy of your neighbours. Most people think that nuclear physics is mainly about creating gigantic mushroom clouds and making vast tracts of land uninhabitable for hundreds of years. In fact there are lots of interesting things to do before you reach that stage.

A particle accelerator is essentially a very handy means of splitting atoms by accelerating sub-atomic particles up to truly amazing speeds and then letting them hit something. They usually consist of a large, circular tube filled with immensely powerful magnets and the main structure can be made by the average handyman by sticking lots of dustbins together with the bottoms cut out. You will need two or three hundred bins, but if your budget won't stretch to this you could economize by joining up old baked bean tins with superglue to make a smaller version.

The main drawback here is that you might not be able to fit big enough magnets inside, but although you will probably not succeed in actually splitting atoms, you should manage to dent them pretty badly and that is almost as much fun. If you build a double track members of the family can have sub-atomic particle races with each other. Incidentally, I should sound a word of warning at this stage. Particle accelerator magnets are very strong indeed and it is not advisable to operate such a device if you have a lot of fillings in your teeth. Going through a line of dustbins at something

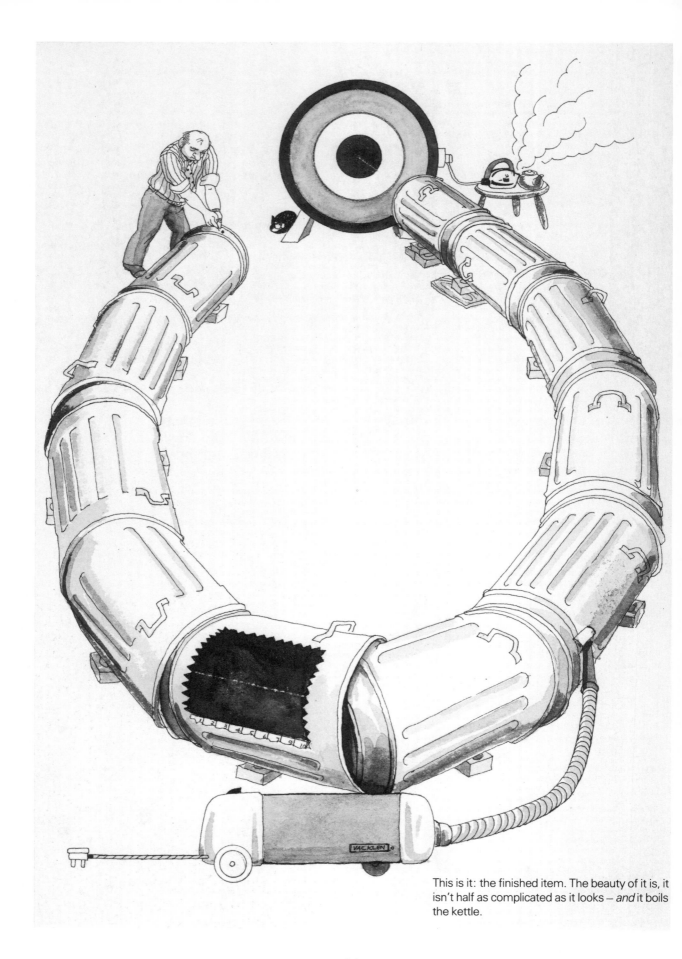

This is it: the finished item. The beauty of it is, it isn't half as complicated as it looks – *and* it boils the kettle.

approaching light speed can seriously damage your health, to say nothing of the dustbins.

At some point in the circle you have made you will need to build in a switching point, so that once your particle has reached maximum velocity you can alter its course to hit the target atom. The cheapest though not necessarily the most accurate way of doing this is to have one of the dustbins temporarily attached to the next. At the appropriate moment you can then rush over, pull the bin out of line and point it at something before the particle comes round again. Do remember that you will have to be very alert as it will be travelling in the region of 150,000 miles per second.

Once your accelerator is ready to run, switch it on and prepare to insert your sub-atomic particle. I should warn your neighbours at this point as the accelerator will probably suck up most of the power in your section of the National Grid and this will affect the little clocks in their video recorders and make them irritable.

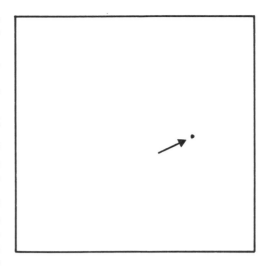

A particle, enlarged 100,000 times under an electron microscope. As you can see, it's still a bit small.

Know Your Particles

The best particles to use are electrons or ions, and in the case of the latter *must not* be confused with steam irons as these are entirely different. Both varieties of particle are absolutely tiny so always use tweezers when handling them.

A particle being selected prior to use in an accelerator. This is a high-precision job.

Tasmanian reader Kenneth O'Gelato sent in this picture of his home-built anti-particle protective suit and helmet. At the moment of firing he reverses the helmet.

a look inside. If everything has worked as it should the atomic nucleus will have been split into little bits of things such as psi-mesons and so on. These should be carefully collected in a matchbox for further study later.

Do experiment a bit. Try accelerating lots of particles at once and seeing how many atoms you can hit at a time. Once you have gained sufficient experience in this field you may wish to go on to put your knowledge to good use and build a proper nuclear reactor. The fission principle is essentially the same but more complex and involves starting a chain reaction with hundreds of nuclei being bombarded at once. The advantages of constructing your own nuclear reactor are enormous and will allow you to start generating your own light and heat.

Fix an old biscuit tin to the end of your accelerator as a reaction chamber and fill it with atoms. Once you fire the first particle into the tin all the atoms will begin colliding with each other and getting very hot. The heat can be used to drive a fan connected to some alternators salvaged from your local car breakers and then, Hey Presto, electricity. You will need to take some elementary precautions as nuclear fission can be a bit dangerous.

For a start you should insulate the reaction tin with lead sheathing. If sheets of this are beyond your means, glueing hundreds of pencils to the outside of the tin will be sufficient. Also, whenever working near the reaction chamber you should wear protective clothing. Failing this, wrap yourself in baking foil from head to toe and wear a diving mask. A more permanent solution would be to save all your old milk bottle tops and sew them to an old suit.

Becoming radioactive is no joke I can tell you. You will know if you have been overexposed because you will start to glow in the dark and this can be most embarrassing. On the plus side it will make walking or cycling after dark much safer on busy roads.

I shouldn't need to remind you that nuclear generators are extremely powerful so do not attempt to connect domestic appliances direct to the power output. Failure to step down the current could lead to your stove going nova or your toast ending up in the attic.

Before inserting the particle you will need to create a vacuum inside the accelerator tube and this can be done quite easily by inserting the upholstery attachment of your vacuum cleaner. You will then be ready to pop in your particle and switch on. Don't expect anything too spectacular; atoms and particles are extremely small and there won't be much of a bang unless you have got something terribly wrong. Either way, there won't be much point in worrying.

Wait a few moments to make sure that the fission has occurred then have

BECAUSE IT'S THERE

← a career in exploring →

How to select an uncharted territory

For those people who feel no desire to pursue great wealth but rather like the idea of being famous, choosing a career that is also a fun hobby can be difficult. One field of human activity which fits the bill perfectly is that of international exploring. You don't need a lot of capital to become a household name for discovering unknown bits of the world. Just try and think of a single famous explorer that isn't well known and you'll see that the possibilities are not impossible.

There are huge areas of the world that are still mysterious, inhabited by strange species who rarely see the light of day. New York's subway is a good example. All you need to get into the international exploration business is a huge pair of khaki shorts, a hat made of cork, a map of some uncharted wastes and a credit card for bribing natives to carry enormous bundles on their heads.

The personal satisfaction can be very considerable for the intrepid explorer who returns triumphant from a journey into the unknown. Crowds will gaze in admiration at the festering sores of some virulent tropical disease as you thumb through the back issues of National Geographic in the waiting room with a knowing smile. Never again will the thought of having to make conversation at a cocktail party cause you sleepless nights or agonized hours trying to hide

behind the curtains. As an explorer you need only gaze wistfully over the heads of the other guests and they will know that your mind is seeing uncharted vistas and remembering the savage joy of facing unimagineable dangers alone.

Where to Go?

Choosing exactly where to start exploring is quite important and can mean the difference between a thrilling adventure and joyous homecoming or dying in a really boring bit of the world without anybody even knowing. The Sahara, for example, is not a good place for a novice explorer to go wandering about. It's not a good place for anybody

The Complete explorer.

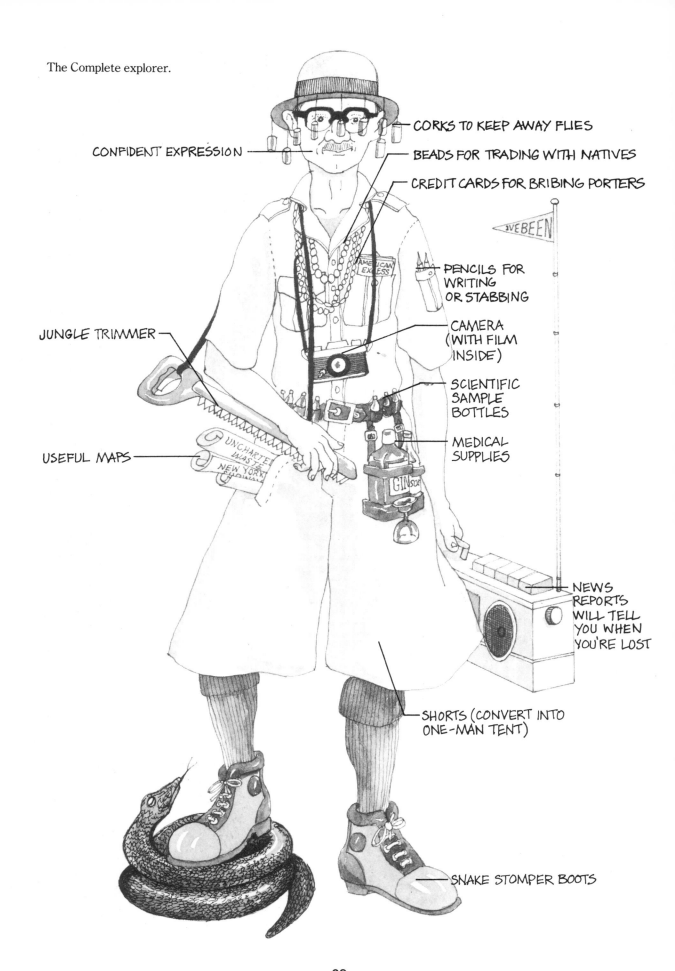

CORKS TO KEEP AWAY FLIES

CONFIDENT EXPRESSION

BEADS FOR TRADING WITH NATIVES

CREDIT CARDS FOR BRIBING PORTERS

AMERICAN EXPRESS

PENCILS FOR WRITING OR STABBING

JUNGLE TRIMMER

CAMERA (WITH FILM INSIDE)

SCIENTIFIC SAMPLE BOTTLES

USEFUL MAPS

UNCHARTED WASTE

NEW YORK SUBWAY

MEDICAL SUPPLIES

GIN

NEWS REPORTS WILL TELL YOU WHEN YOU'RE LOST

SHORTS (CONVERT INTO ONE-MAN TENT)

SNAKE STOMPER BOOTS

really, except hydrophobic beachcombers. Exploring is all about discovering things that no-one else knows about, and everybody, except perhaps Eskimos, knows what sand looks like.

The jungle is the best place to start doing international exploring. Even if one place looks very much like another, you can at least do plenty of hacking your way through slightly impenetrable undergrowth with an electric hedgetrimmer. Just imagine those idyllic moments sitting on a log beside a majestic and unnamed waterfall making nature notes or scrambling up amazingly tall trees as you discover that the log has a very long smile with hundreds of pointy teeth. Every day brings new challenges, every dawn new delights, every night pneumonia.

Essential Kit

Besides those items already mentioned you will need a passport, heavy walking boots for stamping on snakes, a transistor radio for the weather forecast and a box of matches for starting forest fires. A compass is not a good idea as it is just as much fun and certainly less dangerous to keep going round in circles. You never know where you'll end up if you travel in straight lines.

Among your medical supplies should be a considerable quantity of gin and tonic to protect you against malaria. Experienced international explorers drink it all as soon as they arrive, depart for home as soon as the effects wear off and thereby rarely contract this unpleasant disease. You will also need a plentiful supply of sticking plasters and antiseptic to treat lion and tiger bites.

Scientific study is a very important aspect of any expedition into the unknown, and especially the unknown that nobody knows about rather than just the places where you haven't been before. You must take a large supply of small bottles to put hundreds of tiny things in, and tweezers will also be very helpful. They not only help when picking up astonishingly small scientific things, but can be used to remove thorns from wild animal's feet and making them grateful.

Quite a lot of your day in the jungle will be spent rushing about after butterflies and moths to give to zoos. Unless you have unlimited storage space it is best to just collect a single dead specimen of each variety, but do not try and use a gun. Lepidoptera flit about all over the place and unless you are a remarkable shot you may well wipe out the entire expedition. Two ordinary house bricks are perfectly adequate for most species except things like rhinos and elephants who just get incredibly angry.

Keep your socks pulled up to avoid nasty bites from passing mosquitos, crocodiles etc.

Take a Friend

Unless you're very shy, you shouldn't go exploring all on your own. Being intrepid and courageous is rather a waste of time unless there are others to witness it. You need at least one other person in a tent to tell when you decide that you're going outside and might be some time. Incidentally, the historic value of a sentence like that is substantially reduced if you come back again fifteen minutes later.

It's not a bad idea to choose large chubby people to go with you in case you run into cannibals, but not so overweight that you have to push them along all day on a trolley. You will also need to invite at least one girl because proper intrepid explorers never do their own washing. You will need several changes of underwear because unknown jungles are pretty frightening places.

A camera is essential and selling exclusive rights to your photographs can be a good way of paying for your expedition. The pictures which fetch the best prices are unusual wildlife ones of the various creatures in their natural habitat rather than albums full of you putting up the tent or standing with your foot on something dead. Try for those hard-to-get shots like off-duty soldier ants or the insides of hippopotami.

You can hire porters to carry all your gear once you have reached uncharted territory because primitive people like carrying things about, and once you have left civilization far behind there is a good chance that you will encounter undiscovered tribes who would be only too happy to show you round the area slung from stout poles. Their cheerful generosity will probably extend to having you and your team for dinner.

Attractive female explorers can always be traded when the going gets rough.

Nervous explorers of the Kalahari Desert can take some encouragement from the fact that a day-and-night get-you-home service is available.

But however appealing the idea of being a famous explorer may be, the realities of pulling leeches off your tenderest parts or fighting off the attentions of a confused gorilla may not actually be to your taste. It is therefore very sensible to practise a little before setting off into the wilderness. Your local park can serve as an effective training ground to help you get used to stumbling, crazed with thirst, through bushes, trying to get strange animal droppings off your shoes with little pointed sticks, or peering round tree trunks at things without being seen.

THEME PARKS ON A LOW, LOW BUDGET

The theme park concept established by Walt Disney has proved a success for many generations seeking a temporary escape from the realities of everyday life. Amid a carnival atmosphere of colour and excitement, you can slip into any of a number of exotic environments or byegone eras and leave the real world far behind. Hundreds of thousands of people every year pay good money for the experience and more and more new theme parks are being opened as entrepreneurs realise how much profit lies in catering for other people's dreams.

So many, in fact, that the novelty of walking down the main street of Dodge City while goodies and baddies blaze away at each other every hour on the hour, or betting on the outcome as two valiant knights and their caparisoned chargers thunder down the lists, is beginning to wear a little thin. The time has come when for a little ingenuity and a small amount of cash, you too could make a handsome living as a theme park operator.

Starting a small local theme park can provide the same excitement and escapism without the need to travel miles to get to one of the large and usually very crowded traditional theme parks. To start with you could even make use of your own house and garden to provide facilities that are new and unusual.

Your greenhouse will provide the basis for a wildlife or jungle safari ride. Members of the family can take it in turns with the wheelbarrow to carry small parties through the steaming tangle of exotic undergrowth while cats, dogs and budgerigars dart hither and thither in Nature's ceaseless game of survival. A few strategically placed electric kettles will lend atmosphere as your visitors push their way through the dense green wall of tomato plants to the saucer of water that dominates the wildlife reserve area. Pause here for refreshments in the carefully concealed hide from which woodlice, earwigs and worms can be photographed in their natural habitat. Then under the lawn sprinkler for a taste of the monsoon season and on to the next experience.

Spacewalk
Your garage can provide a glimpse into the future and it's all aboard for a ride to the stars. Hear the mighty revving of old lawnmower engines as visitors strap

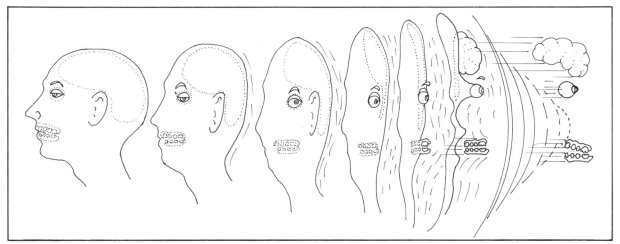

There's a lot fo G-force about in theme parks. The third stage from the left represents what happens to your face at 142G. It's not really safe to go beyond that but you can always try.

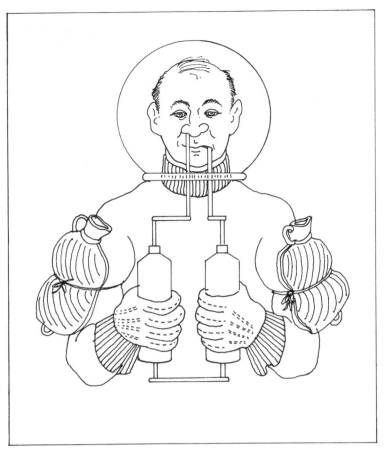

Respirator outfit with vital pressure pads on arms. Squeeze right hand to flood nostril with air, squeeze left to extract – and so on. This is an unfiltered recirculation system, not to be used for more than a few minutes if you want to avoid feeling unwell, or worse.

themselves into their deckchairs and enjoy a space-meal of powdered milk and boiled sweets. A sharp tug on the string tied to the supports of each chair and they will experience the bewildering thrust of G-force as the space clipper surges into the sky. Then they are free of Earth's atmosphere and wholly dependent on the old washing-up liquid bottles and straws for their air supply.

Stars, moons and mysterious planets rush past the windows as fast as your children can run without falling over and tearing the drawings. At the climax of the flight you can warn them of an impending meteorite shower through the tin cans and string with which each passenger has been equipped. White-knuckled hands grasp the seats as scores of speeding pebbles rattle on the roof and windows. When you have reached your destination a stout cord attached to a ringbolt in the ceiling and the back of your

trousers will let you drift weightlessly past the passengers, bidding each a spacetraveller's farewell. Do make sure that there is someone to catch you at the opposite end of the garage as it is terribly hard looking like Flash Gordon or Luke Skywalker travelling backwards into shelves of paint and old tools.

Jet lag special
How about an international tour in which customers can savour the flavour of a dozen countries in as many minutes. As soon as the party is assembled it's off to Paris for a quick walk round an accordion dressed in onions, and if the weather is nice and damp, a snack of snails and frogs' legs. Off with the berets and on with the lederhosen and blowing tubas for a taste of the Munich Beer Festival, then it's dressing gowns and bowing for the inscrutable East. In the interests of safety make sure that there is sufficient space when

bowing starts to avoid the embarrassment of multiple concussions.

Wind up the thermostat, swear loudly and extravagantly and don your Jaws costume for a quick trip round Australia before handing out the sheets and standing in buckets of sand under the Sahara's blazing sunlamp. Sprint through the greenhouse before the next safari party comes through and then it's off to the freezer for the wastelands of Siberia. By now your party may be suffering the effects of jet lag so allow them out into the garden for a relaxing stroll round an English country garden.

No round-the-world trip would be complete without a visit to the skyscrapers of New York but they will have to take it in turns going up a really long ladder to get the feel of it. Borrow a yellow car and hurtle up and down the street before dropping them off behind the house for a quick mugging to empty their wallets.

Yes, the fantasy park in your garage could look like this – a whistlestop tour of many nations with a submarine trip and a supermarket-trolley derby thrown in.

People always dream of living a different kind of life from their own so you are on to a winner if you let parties of manual workers spend a happy hour or two talking into rows of surplus telephones and moving pieces of paper around on trestle tables. The office workers can run happily into the street and make big holes with pickaxes and whistle at girls to their hearts' content.

However excitingly original your theme park may be there will always be a few unimaginative individuals who only want to take a drink in a genuine Western bar or gorge themselves at an Elizabethan banquet. To avoid the need to take on extra staff and to make the most efficient use of your resources, you could satisfy such customers by combining the two.

Every visitor is issued with a doublet and hose, ten-gallon hat, codpiece and holster and is invited to enjoy a rowdy drink in the minstrels' gallery while Apaches sing madrigals and dance around the roasting ox. When dinner is ready they tuck into a grand feast of stuffed peacock and beans washed down with horns of corn liquor as a jester juggles branding irons and dulcimers. Guests are encouraged to join in and throw their bones to the festive coyotes in keeping with the spirit of the occasion. When the time has come for them to leave, you could present each with a facsimile copy of 'Greensleeves' and a realistic nylon scalp as mementos of their participation.

The possibilities for themes around which to construct your theme park are almost unlimited. Among those which are most economic to set up are Doctor's Waiting Room Relay, Supermarket Trolley Grand Prix and Submarine Adventure (although you should bear in mind that this may well be outside your washing machine guarantee). In addition to the main events you should provide a good range of games and activities like Stuffing Pound Notes Through the Letterbox. Theme parks tend to be quite noisy, boisterous places so if you value peace and quiet it is advisable to keep a list of your aquaintances' holiday dates in order to plan opening times and venues.

Here's a cheap idea. One punter sits at wheel and the other does the shooting. You provide the old car, hats, gun, noise and rocking motion.

Fringe & Fridge medicine

Some New Directions

As doctor's surgeries become increasingly overcrowded and waiting lists for treatment grow ever longer, more and more people are turning to practitioners of fringe medicine for help. This has created wonderful opportunities for the compassionate and socially aware to amass huge piles of surplus cash.

The really good thing about fringe medicine is that you don't have to spend years cutting up dead people and reading enormous books to start making money. All you need is some space, an earnest expression and some white overalls in case a patient bleeds or is violently sick. A collection of obscure pieces of paper, such as old share certificates or income tax returns, framed and hung on the walls will lend an air of authority to your garage.

Fringe medicine is not to be confused with **fridge medicine** or cryogenics, and has almost nothing to do with hair-care. It covers two main areas; bodily health and psychological well-being, and if you enjoy either of these you could be eligible to practise. If you have neither you could also be eligible.

Before deciding upon your field you must have a good look around at the options and try some of them out on your friends and elderly relatives. Here are a few to consider:

Amputism The basic idea of this doctrine is to cut off any bits of the human body that are not working properly. It requires the minimum of skill, but when treating recurring headaches it is wise to insist on payment in advance. An advantage of this field is that no-one else is doing it so there is very little competition.

Armpitism No-one's working in this field either and I think you ought to keep it that way.

Acupuncture In this rapidly expanding field of fringe medicine disorders are treated by impaling the patient with enormous needles poked into tender parts of the body. The effectiveness of the system is illustrated by the fact that few

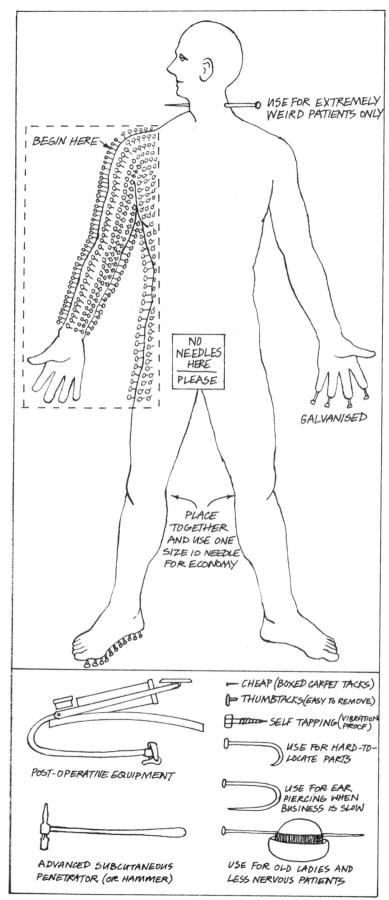

USE FOR EXTREMELY WEIRD PATIENTS ONLY

BEGIN HERE

NO NEEDLES HERE PLEASE

GALVANISED

PLACE TOGETHER AND USE ONE SIZE 10 NEEDLE FOR ECONOMY

POST-OPERATIVE EQUIPMENT

ADVANCED SUBCUTANEOUS PENETRATOR. (OR HAMMER)

— CHEAP (BOXED CARPET TACKS)

THUMBTACKS (EASY TO REMOVE)

SELF TAPPING (VIBRATION PROOF)

USE FOR HARD-TO-LOCATE PARTS

USE FOR EAR PIERCING WHEN BUSINESS IS SLOW

USE FOR OLD LADIES AND LESS NERVOUS PATIENTS

Beginner's acupuncture chart and useful kit.

patients return a second time. The choice of needles is very important. They should be long enough to reach those parts that conventional medicine fails to reach, yet not so long as to nail the patient to the couch. Unless, of course, they are very, very angry indeed.

Hatpins are ideal for the beginner as they are fairly inexpensive and you can use both hands to drive them home. They should always be properly dried after use as they do tend to rust if not cared for. This problem can be avoided altogether by using galvanized roofing nails.

Finding the correct spot to insert your needles does require quite a lot of practice so the novice should begin by covering the entire body area to make certain. Once the operation is over, the patient should be re-inflated to about 26psi using a sterile foot-pump or airline.

Chiropractice This is anatomical origami in which patients are folded into complex shapes without cutting or tearing them. The trick is knowing just how small to get them without snapping bits off. A chiropracter's skill is measured by the number and volume of the popping noises that usually accompany this technique but it does take quite a lot of practice before you can detonate patients correctly. In the meantime a novice can impress his clients by stewing moist kelp beneath the couch. A bit of fancy footwork as you manipulate your patient will create a favourable impression. Balloons are not a suitable substitute unless you are an expert at dealing with cardiac arrest.

Electrotherapy The use of electricity to stimulate the body's own remedial processes is starting to regain some of its earlier popularity. The idea is to pass sizeable charges through affected portions of the body to stimulate the nervous, vascular and lymphatic systems. In fact even just the sight of forty tons of gleaming Van de Graaf generator is often enough to do the trick.

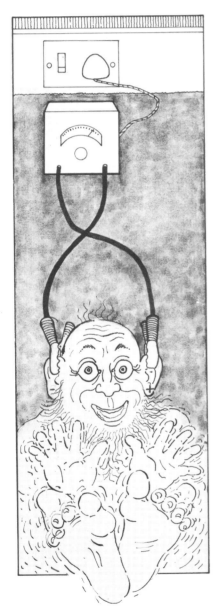

Low-voltage current from a household battery charger is usually quite enough for our more senior citizens, but do get them to sign the release forms before treatment as their hands are a bit shaky afterwards.

It is worth seating waiting patients in the actual treatment room as miraculous cures can be effected on entire groups at a time. The sight of a previously lethargic or geriatric patient break dancing furiously on the end of a three-core, heavy duty cable can make everybody feel so much better in seconds.

Equipment of this standard is certainly expensive and may well be beyond the means of the novice electro-therapist. If this is the case you can make a start treating minor ailments such as hangovers or ingrowing toenails by getting your clients to lick torch batteries. DO NOT ask them to stick their tongues into mains sockets. This is dangerous and silly.

Homeopathy A homeopath is someone who has an irrational fear of houses, particularly their own. Although this condition is extremely difficult to treat effectively, you can make quite a lot of money by charging them rent to stay in your garden.

Herbalism This is the treatment of physical ailments through a diet of ground-up shrubs and aromatic plants. The raw materials are quite expensive but it is a fashionable approach to healthcare so you can charge a great deal. It is possible to combine traditional herbalism with the current vogue for high fibre diets by encouraging your clients to eat the various shrubs whole. Making and marketing your own range of medications is an extremely rewarding aspect of this branch of fringe medicine. Things like sugar-coated fir cones are cheap to produce and really make your clients feel that they are getting value for money. You can then charge even more to get them out again.

Electrotherapy can also be used to thaw meat straight from the freezer.

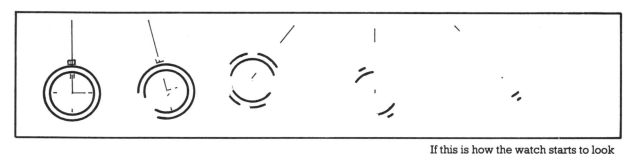

If this is how the watch starts to look to you when you're hypnotising stop at once and try another way.

Massage Though not strictly a branch of fringe medicine, massage is a useful addition to the practitioner's range of skills. The correct technique is not difficult to accomplish, and entails pouring oil over someone and smacking them really hard until they pay you money. The problem is that certain elements have brought the practice into considerable disrepute and it now has some rather seedy connotations. To avoid any possibility of suspicion, tie rubber gloves filled with porridge or jelly to the ends of long bamboo poles. If you slide these through the window and stand in full view of the neighbours you should put paid to any potential scandal.

Hypnotism This is another technique gaining in popularity which can prove lucrative through convincing patients that they are allergic to their wallets. It takes a little practice to become proficient but it is worth persevering. Stand in front of a mirror like this, and dangle a bright object in front of the eyes. As it swings to and fro, whisper "You are feeling very sleepy, very sleepy. You can hardly keep your eyes ....

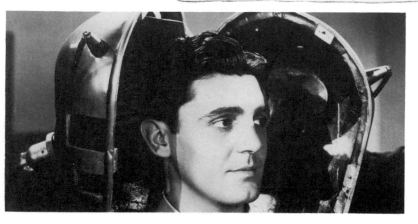

In home massage, working through a modesty screen (two holes are usually sufficient) will avoid unpleasant scandal. Advertise your trade with rubber gloves.

Big money can be made by using this latest machine for the removal of unwanted facial hair. It's easy to operate but must be carefully adjusted for each client to avoid removal of eyelashes, eyebrows and head hair.

TURN FIBRE INTO FUEL WITH YOUR OWN BODILY FUNCTIONS

Any responsible person living in this age of fast food, rapid depletion of natural resources, and sudden death through enjoying yourself, must give serious thought to the way in which life is approached. If you are rich and careless of anything that does not immediately afford you pleasure you run a deadly risk of living a long and happy life, and everybody knows that this is very unhealthy and wholly unnatural.

Living is a deadly serious business and the thinking person must take far more responsibility for his/her own health and way of life. The rewards are immeasurable and overwhelming and I won't go into them now. Suffice it to say that they are huge and quite numerous and sometimes of fairly significant advantage and can occasionally slightly improve your quality of life if you're very, very lucky.

Let's take health for a start and anybody's will do so grab as much as you can before they notice. Modern foods, though sometimes absolutely delicious and packed with health-giving properties, are by definition modern foods and therefore not appropriate for a body that is based on an antiquated design.

There are two ways of tackling this problem. The first is to revise your diet to include only antiquated food, and the second is to modernize your body. Neither is much fun which is why slim people never look as content as those who are overweight and certain to die eventually. If it were lots of fun you might just as well carry on eating and drinking and buying petrol.

This is what fibre looks like before you put the milk and sugar on.

Having established that misery is essential for a happy life we must totally revise our eating habits and the most important aspect is the question of roughage. Because the diet of primitive peoples naturally contains a

39

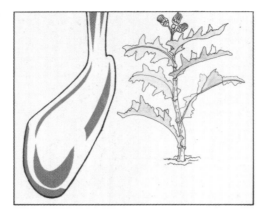

Weed flicking is a healthy outdoor exercise. You don't *have* to eat all the weeds.

Just look at the difference between this battery-produced egg and the free-range egg beside it. Now you can see why one is so much more nutritious than the other.

high proportion of roughage, they never have to go into hospital to have babies and can just produce them sitting down in bushes. The first step in changing your diet is therefore to rip up the brick-paved patio and plant a wide range of shrubs so that you will not embarrass the neighbours when the roughage does its work and the garden fills with children.

Roughage can be found in most non-processed foods such as cabbage stalks, wholewheat and coconut matting and should be incorporated into every meal. Wholewheat is the most commonly employed wholefood and is called this because you are required to eat the whole thing, baling twine and all. Roughage acts as a natural means of cleansing the body by forming a solid wad like a sort of drainrod. Teeth marks on a bathroom doorhandle are the sign of a healthy wholefood family.

Eggs found lying in the grass are another healthy food especially if eaten with their shells on. Remember, nothing should be taken away from natural foods and they should be eaten with the minimum preparation. Admittedly some things like oranges or melons can momentarily bring tears to the eyes but the body will soon adapt. There are exceptions — otherwise no-one would have thought of the microwave — and cows and sheep fall into this category.

Generally speaking, the more horrible the food the better it is for you, like medicine. As a result the healthiest, most invigorating food in the whole world is junket, but not many people want to be *that* healthy. Junket is closely followed by home-made yoghurt, which should be positively boiling and writhing with rampant goodness, but do not make too much at a time as it can be dangerous in large gangs.

The second approach, modernizing your body, is based on lots of the right kind of exercise which means plenty of invigorating repetition. Variety is the enemy of modern health which is why jogging is acknowledged as being the best possible way of training the mind not to interfere with the process of becoming healthy by experiencing stimuli, and the body to realize that its only task is to keep going irrespective of where it's going to. Static exercises such as sit-ups are intended to train the muscles to act of their own accord, so that, in the unthinkable event of time catching up with you, you might die but you probably won't lie down.

But health is only one aspect of modern thinking. Self-sufficiency is the second philosophy of the responsible person, and begins with energy conservation. Having become acceptably indignant about the squandering of the Earth's fossil fuels, the next step is reorganizing your domestic environment to make use of alternative sources of energy. Taurus poo, you might say, and you will certainly be on the right track, for animals' waste products are coming up from behind in the race for the fuel of the future.

How To Make Methane

The reason is that these unsavoury items are rich in methane, which burns wonderfully well and provides sufficient heat to keep out the chill of winter nights as well as drive

Lady guests at Dingly Dell Health Farm wait for the word before getting stuck into their lunchtime bananas. The waiting looks agonizing.

Like most great ideas, ever so simple: a foolproof device for collecting valuable methane gas from sheep, known to produce 123 litres of the fuel each day. When the sheep is airborne, it's time to disconnect the bag.

41

Models demonstrate optimum position for methane expulsion. Note use of facial musculature and hands over ears to prevent sonar damage.

Purified methane under 15 atmospheres of pressure.

domestic appliances and even motor cars. However, in the latter instance you may find that everyone else on the road throws caution to the wind in order to overtake you and the exhaust fumes that *you* are throwing to the wind.

Unfortunately, it is not as simple as unloading your pooper-scooper in the grate and setting fire to it. Elaborate systems have to be constructed in order to allow the waste matter to deteriorate sufficiently to release the methane, which is then collected in milk bottles and stored in the fridge until required. Do not despair if you lack the money or expertise to equip yourself with the necessary paraphernalia. A workable substitute, although it will not give you the same volume of methane, is to tie plastic bags on to the rear quarters of available animals.

A diet of beans, mashed artichokes and raw cabbage will generate enough for a small household. This system can be applied to pet dogs, cats and even budgerigars, and if you wish to increase methane production still further, to you and your family. In this case you *must* remember not to sit down too heavily when visiting other households. If for no other reason than that methane is highly inflammable, the detonation of the plastic bag could cause cardiac arrest in someone who has not taken the early part of this chapter to heart. To say nothing of the effect on your trousers.

Wind power is also an important source of energy, and this has nothing to do with the preceding paragraphs. By equipping your home with a huge propeller you can generate sufficient electricity for your needs. If it fails to do so you can really rev it up and move your house to somewhere where electricity is cheaper or more readily available.

Solar power is not really worth considering because of the vast clouds of methane which are beginning to obscure the sun.

A windpower installation designed to power a 40-watt light bulb. To light two bulbs, simply double up the system.

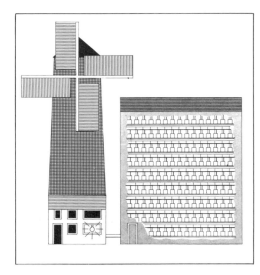

GENETICS?
That's Your Breeding Business

Genetics can be both fascinating and financially rewarding but is certainly not for the prudish as it is all to do with ... you know ... parts of the body involved in breeding and stuff. Hence the name, and as your biology teacher should have explained, we all have genetics and they are nothing to be ashamed of. But when I say that there is money to be made from it, there is no need to start getting all peculiar about it, because I don't mean that you have to become a person of the night or anything.

It is something that can be done with plants and animals as well as people and is all perfectly above board. A monk called Mendel discovered that by mixing up jeans he could get sweet peas to grow in different colours. Who would have guessed that from such pointless beginnings it would become possible to create amazingly hairy cats and completely hairless dogs! And all in the space of a few hundred years.

Well, so much for the history of genetics. These days genetic engineering became the thing of the future ages ago and the techniques are no longer a mystery. With very simple equipment and the minimum of skill, you too can begin manipulating genes for fun and profit. The first thing to do is to learn the basic techniques.

Inside every living cell is a blueprint or 'memory' of what the cell belongs to and if you want to change this you must get it very confused. Hypnotism is a good method but time consuming, particularly with plants. It is much better to isolate a particular cell and put it in the company of lots of cells of a different kind. For example, put a cell from a black rabbit with lots of white rabbit cells and it gets mixed up and makes a black and white rabbit. To take this a stage further, if you mix the black and white rabbit cell with frog spawn you will get a fluffy black and white frog that eats carrots.

Using tweezers, a plentiful supply of old yoghurt pots and your oven set to a nice low heat, you can start inventing useful and interesting life-forms. Limit your work to plants to start with

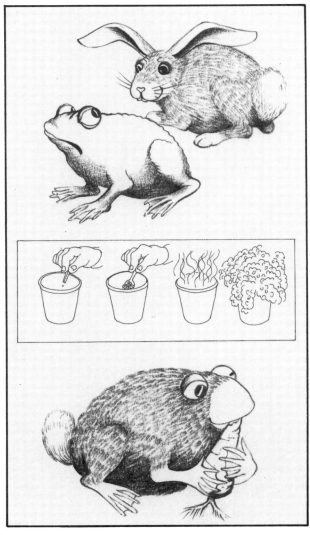

A successful outcome to an experiment involving breeding a rabbit with a frog by means of cell culture. Keep the tweezers clean if you want to avoid unexpected genetic developments.

as they are much simpler. Lots of people talk with their plants, except of course Continentals who talk with their hands instead, and this does help to calm them before an operation. Try to keep the subject matter simple as plants are not renowned for their intellectual prowess.

Then, when they are not expecting it, rush up and pull out a few cells and pop them in your yoghurt pots full of jelly. After a few hours in the warm oven you should be able to hear them multiplying and can begin mixing them up. But don't just do it willy-nilly because you might end up with Triffids that will eat you out of house and home.

Selective breeding can produce prize specimens that will be a useful addition to the home. A giant Venus flytrap can be a great deal cheaper than a waste-disposal unit and much more fun. The digestive juices it secretes can be exploited to bring a sheen to your silverware that will be the envy of your friends. Suddenly you're in business.

Once you have gained experience with plants you can really start to make big money by turning

An unsuccessful outcome to Prof Irving Nosepicker's experiment in which he tried to breed a cross between a daffodil and a python. After this, his 47th failure, the professor took up dentistry.

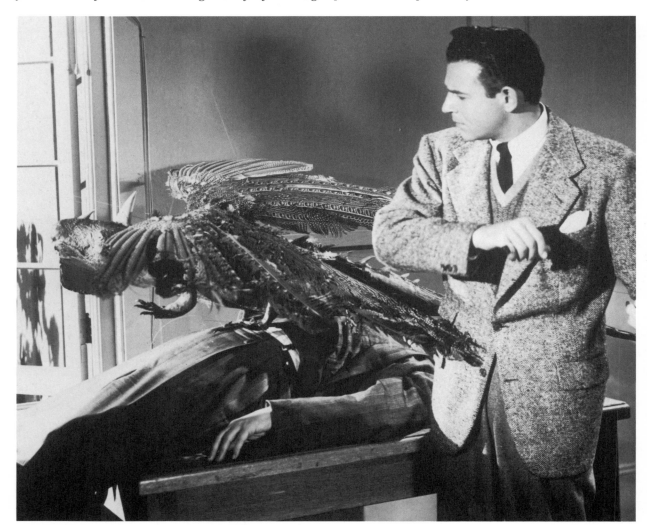

Genetics can have its nasty moments. Dr Walter Pentacle was suddenly attacked by his mutant sparrow and was only saved by the timely intervention of his tax advisor, who wishes to remain anonymous.

It took top scientists a good few years to evolve the monster assault tortoise though the basic theory is pretty simple, as the cell system at the top shows.

Another case of genetic engineering getting out of control.
This is the famous case of Lord Bunter's butler, who
unwisely ate what he thought was a jelly but was actually
a jelly culture on its way to becoming a playmate for Lord
Bunter's ape.

to the animal kingdom. For example cross-breeding electric eels with porcupines will enable you to churn out hundreds of toasted marshmallows for a child's birthday party without having to light a fire. If you have a fancy for setting up in the rag trade why not cross-breed sheep and silkworms and then sit back and watch your flocks churning out next season's knitwear collection. Or cross crickets with bats and go into the sports goods business.

The really big international money is in arms and military equipment and that has been covered in some depth in one of my earlier books (*Do-it-Yourself Brain Surgery and Other Home Skills*). But there are other possibilities besides Combat Hamsters, Blitzkrieg Armadillos and Magnetically Triggered Cod. How about the

Monster Assault Tortoise for example? This magnificent specimen is inexpensive to produce but offers the awesome capability of wiping out acres of lettuces in a single day and starving the enemy into submission.

The market is not getting any easier, however, and modern troops are able to command considerable firepower. Strength and defensive armour are sometimes not enough and it is worth considering other approaches to today's battlefield situations. Genetic engineering can make a valuable contribution in this area and entirely new weapons can be evolved. Can you imagine, for example, the effect on even the most battle-hardened enemy troops if they suddenly found themselves under attack from several dozen forty-foot pink fluffy bunnies all bounding over the top at once. If these were supported by raucous squadrons of giant parrots with an inbred digestive disorder a complete rout would be a foregone conclusion.

HANDS OFF MAGGOTS !

conservation in the home

Possibly the simplest way to encourage wildlife in the home.

Protecting the interests of dumb animals against human exploitation has never been more fashionable. Almost any social gathering means an ordeal of shame and tortured conscience if you are not sending trees to restore the rain forests of South America or knitting pullovers for elephants suffering from the climatic changes brought about by aerosol deodorants.

But not everyone can afford to devote their weekends to ramming Russian whalers or tearing up fur coats. For some it is enough of a financial struggle looking after a family without trying to **sponsor a gorilla** through a secretarial college. But if you are fed up with dodging rabid tin-rattlers every Saturday morning, do not despair.

There is a huge section of the world's flora and fauna which has been subjected to an unpublicized war of attrition for countless years. For the minimum outlay and in the comfort of your own home, you can become a champion of the voiceless oppressed. You too can embark on a conservation crusade and sneer at the unenlightened by declaring your house a conservation area.

The average house is the natural world in microcosm. A host of innocent life-forms endure wholesale and mindless slaughter as they eke out a precarious living in a hostile environment. A delicate ecological balance is constantly at risk and desperately needs your help to survive.

With little effort and even less expense you can form your own Animal Action Group and wear **'Save a Silverfish Today'** badges. Slugs, bluebottles, earwigs, woodlice, cockroaches and rats play an important part in a complex and exciting natural cycle in which you can play a vital role. By fostering the conditions necessary to their lifestyles you can enjoy the social benefits of being shrill and earnest in public.

A few small changes in your domestic routines can bring peace and happiness to our tiny brethren. Throw away those cruel chemical cleansers, sell that vile vacuum cleaner, disconnect your toilet cistern and watch grateful life blossom around you.

Why waste those chop bones, bacon rinds and chicken carcases when you can provide an vital source of nourishment for our little friends by tucking them under the sofa or behind the radiators? Even family pets can make a valuable contribution if you throw away Fido's leash and brick up the cat-flap.

By designating your living room an area of outstanding natural beauty you will have the immense satisfaction of seeing life flourish in its wild and natural state. What was once nothing more than an unwanted slice of quiche is now a joyous mound of **fit and glistening maggots** tumbling in the playfulness of youth.

That heap of unwashed underwear under the coffee table has been transformed into a riot of funghal colour that will amaze the casual visitor. Boredom will be a thing of the past as the family gazes in awe at the setting sun gleaming on the sea of silverfish that ebbs and flows around the furniture.

Why not involve the whole family in this exciting and rewarding adventure? Each member could choose their own conservation project and help other households to join in saving these many threatened species. Here are some suggestions to get you started.

An Indoor Mould Garden

There is little to compare with a flourishing and rampant mould garden for colour and variety, and the easiest way to get started is to stock up your refrigerator with a good selection of foods

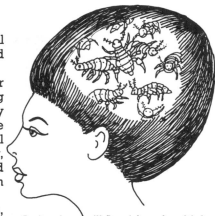

A nit colony will flourish and multiply if left undisturbed.

rich in fats and protein and then turn off the power. Within a few days the first delicate blooms will appear, filling the air with their tiny spores. Once the colony has become firmly established it will spread rapidly across the floor and walls. Suede-look wallpaper effects can be simply achieved by applying a thin film of butter with a paint roller.

Even more dramatic effects can be obtained by penetrating the damp-proof membrane with a drill in several places or making a few small holes in your water tank. This will allow a splendid variety of magnificent funghi to alter the contours of your rooms.

If you prefer something rather more subtle, why not encourage a secret mould garden in the linen cupboard, oven or spare bedroom. This will allow guests to make their own glorious discoveries.

Start a Rat Herd

A regular source of food and a warm, secure refuge are the most important ingredients for starting your own rat herd. These criteria are most easily satisfied by making a slit along the sides of your mattress and inserting unwanted food. A healthy breeding pair of young adults can then be introduced into their new home and within a very short time the warmth of your body will help to nurture the first, thrilling litter. You will be amazed at the speed with which a good sized herd can be created. Within weeks you will be lulled to sleep by the

chittering and squeaking of scores of contented rodents. Mealtimes will become especially exciting as a brown furry tide scampers into the room to strip your plates bare in seconds.

A Nit or Louse Colony

Providing a sanctuary for these persecuted creatures is a good project for mums and daughters and the household budget will benefit from the absence of shampoo and razorblades from the shopping list. Start by fashioning your hair into the 'beehive' style so popular in the sixties. Provided that the hair is then left completely undisturbed for a few months, there is a good chance these friendly insects will establish themselves in their new home. You will then be in the enviable position of being able to show your own contribution whenever the topic of conservation arises.

Maggot Sanctuary

This is another ideal project for the novice which can yield spectacular results, not least because of the variety of stages in the life cycle of the maggot. The remnants of the Sunday joint provide a perfect starting point if left on the lawn for a few hours before placing on the central heating boiler. Before long the first little white snout will emerge to begin life's great adventure. But this is not all, for within days your home will shimmer with the brilliant hues of the adult bluebottle, the humming bird of the insect world, as flocks dart and glitter from room to room amid the soothing hum of ongoing life.

Of course, feeding flocks of this size becomes easier if you enlist the support of your conservation-minded local butcher. He will probably be able to let you have the odd cow or pig that has gone past its sell-by date for next to nothing. One good carcass in the living room will

Just a few ideas for turning your lounge into a bustling nature reserve.

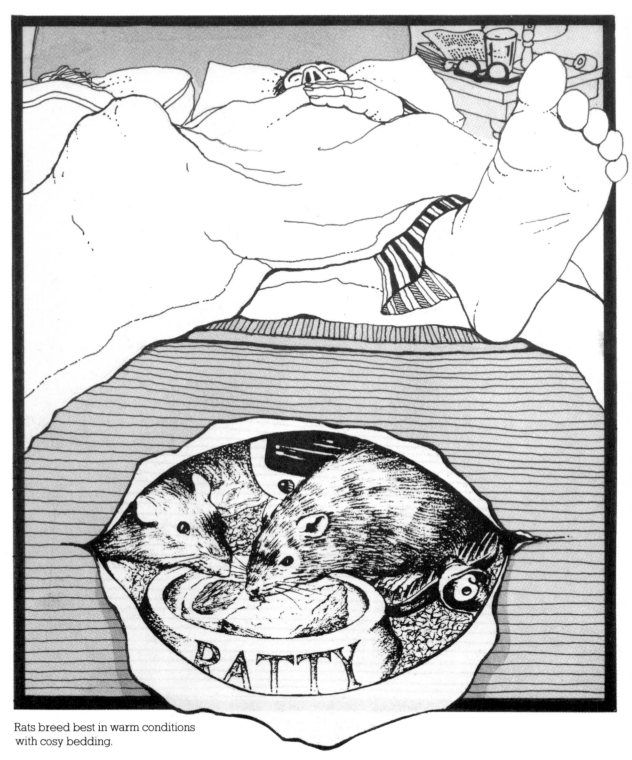

Rats breed best in warm conditions with cosy bedding.

last for several generations of this irridescent insect.

Self Sufficiency

As each project matures you will find that colonies of healthy creatures become less dependent on your help and free you for other wildlife schemes such as establishing a bathroom sluggery. And there are many hidden benefits. Why, for example, go to all the trouble and expense of tiling a shower cubicle when could it be encrusted with softly gleaming snails from floor to ceiling? Why insulate the roof with expensive fibre when it could be inches deep in heat retaining bat droppings? Nature is bountiful to those who show mercy and compassion, and the small outlay involved in such schemes is more than offset by the money you'll save on entertaining your fellow man.

Be a Billionaire Boffin With Home Inventing

Everyone gets tremendous satisfaction from creating something wholly original even if it isn't really, and that's what inventing is all about. The secret is to be the first to put your name to something that everybody else could have thought of if they'd had the time. Take Leonardo da Vinci for example. Practically everybody knows what a parachute is and therefore no-one bothered to draw one until he had a go and became famous overnight as an inventor.

Realizing the enormous potential, he then went on to draw lots of other things like tanks and airplanes and naked men and thereby secured a place in history as the father of military equipment, air travel and nudism. What's more, he didn't actually have to build anything to be credited with the glory. He simply sold the drawings he did for a small fortune and was able to retire and devote himself to painting enigmatic smiles.

But don't make the mistake of thinking that it's too easy. Getting flashes of inspiration takes quite a lot of practice and you need to get your brain in good condition. There are various inventor's exercises that will help, and making sure that your brain has a plentiful supply of blood is very important. Every now and then throughout the day, you should pivot abruptly from the hips to swing your head between your ankles, then up again and repeat the process going backwards. This throws the blood to the inventing parts of the brain. Don't do this exercise too forcibly without placing adhesive tape over the eyes to stop them popping out.

After a while you will probably find your own favourite inventing positions. Some people have even invented inventions to help the process. Archimedes decided that he did his very best deliberating in warm, soapy water so he lay down and invented the bath. Isaac Newton preferred sitting under trees and throwing apples into the air, and to save having to have a huge pile of apples, he invented gravity so that he could use the same one over and over again. Stephenson always thought best on trains so he invented the Rocket. Whatever technique you decide will suit *you* best should be relaxing and free from distractions. If

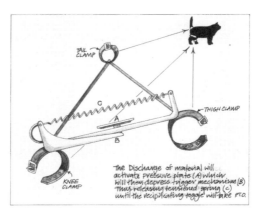

This effective device for the rapid transferral of unwanted cat (or dog) waste was invented by yours truly. Any offers will be considered.

A simple exercise to get the blood rushing to your head and thus increase your brain power. Tape your eyes in to stop them popping out.

below
Regimental Sergeant
Major Nobby Wiggins
invented the cottage loaf
while doodling at a
streetside cafe table.
Here he is seen showing
his working drawings to
an excited baker.

below right
Enzo Cannelloni won first
prize at the 1957
Chittagong Inventors
Festival for this radio-
controlled mobile pulpit
and drinks dispenser,
which functions equally
well in the Northern
Hemisphere.

you wish to take inventing seriously you should begin by giving up your job and spending all your time in bed in a darkened room until money-making ideas begin to appear.

There is very little you will need in the way of actual equipment until you get onto inventing really complicated things like robot cat-tray emptiers or pneumatic apple corers. A pencil and paper are essential and you will have to develop your drawing ability so that others can be really amazed at your genius. The best idea in the world is useless if your representation of it resembles a bowl of spaghetti in a tumble drier.

Your early inventions are unlikely to earn you a lot of money as they should be basically the discovery of vague concepts in order to get your brain working along the right lines. Start with things like A Theory for the Origin of Life and the Universe or The Importance of Soap Operas for Directing Self-Determination in Developing Third World Countries. Once you have learned the basic skills and have acquired a reputation as a potential genius you can begin to turn your powerful mind to resolving some of the real problems of day to day life. That is when the big money starts to roll in.

Once you are ready to progress from dreaming up generalized concepts to inventing actual usable objects, there are two ways of setting about it. You can either invent something and then try and find a use

Do try not to let things get out of proportion. This is undoubtedly an excellent machine for heating up your shaving water, but isn't it a bit big? It's a golden rule that every inventor must occasionally step back from his creation and ask himself whether it really makes sense.

far left
For every acceptance letter there are bound to be ten (or more) rejection slips. Our model shows how to grit your teeth, jut your jaw and take it on the chin.

left
This sad, lonely robot has remained inert since found abandoned on a Scottish moor in 1982. Surely someone will give him a home. It would only be a matter of time and patience before you got him going and found out what he can do.

for it, or you can isolate a social need and create something to satisfy it. Splitting atoms is an example of the first philosophy (see *Build Your Own Particle Accelerator*). After discovering that it could be done, and inventing the equipment to achieve it, the originators looked for novel ways to exploit the new process such as making enormous bangs and huge clouds of smoke.

On the other hand, you may have noticed that whenever someone's dog disgraces himself in the dining room during a social function, the offending animal is hauled bodily from the room and thrown outside. This is tedious and can badly disrupt the flow of social intercourse. There is an obvious opportunity here for the aspiring inventor to turn his mind to solving a common problem by making it unnecessary to haul the offending animal from the house.

He could, perhaps, devise a miniature catapult that can be attached to the creature's nether regions. The dog would then be removed from the house before the guests start arriving and the catapult will hurl the material in question through the dining room window from the garden. Thus the disruptive need to drag the dog through a roomful of guests is deftly avoided. This is an example of the second approach.

Finding further applications for existing inventions is also a worthwhile pursuit. The world cries out for more efficient exploitation of resources, so why not bend your creative energies to inventing a washing machine attachment for a domestic electric drill or a miniature hydro-electric generator for your bathtap to reduce those crippling household electricity bills. Some ideas in this area can achieve spectacular results for very little outlay, such as manufacturing a roller covered in suction cups to replace the roller on your vacuum cleaner for removing old floor tiles or wallpaper. Or how about a device to reverse the polarity of the waste disposal unit of a domestic sink to provide the luxury of a jacuzzi for your household pets?

All the above suggestions come under the heading of mechanical inventions and a whole new area of

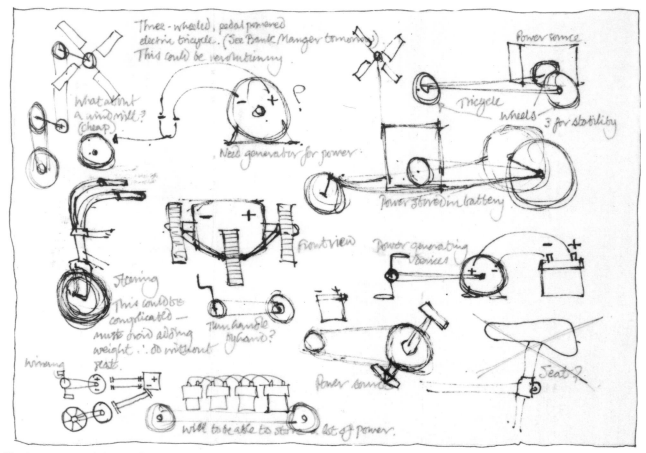

The following handwritten notes appear on the sketch:

Three-wheeled, pedal powered electric tricycle. (See Bank Manager tomorrow). This could be very interesting

What about a windmill? (cheap)

Need generator for power

Power source

Tricycle wheels — 3 for stability

Power stored in battery

Front view

Power generating devices

Steering. This could be complicated — must avoid adding weight ∴ do without seat.

Turn handle by hand?

wiring

Power source

Will to be able to store a lot of power.

Seat?

The importance of clear and accurate drawing cannot be overstressed. This started as a promising idea for a pedal-assisted electric tricycle but the inventor's confused thinking at the drawing stage let him down. I mean, honestly, he hasn't even used a ruler.

possibilities has been opened up through advances in the field of electronics. The microchip has brought a new lease on life to the inventor and has made possible such social benefits as the digital doormat that tears the shoes off anyone who fails to wipe their feet or the electronic hairbrush that gives you a print-out so you can chart your hair loss.

Almost every area of human activity offers the inventor a chance to make his unique contribution. The world of sport waits with bated breath for the arrival of the metal-rimmed racing wheel to reduce the time lost through punctures, and the electronically guided tennis ball which stays inside the court to avoid unpleasant arguments.

The entertainment industry awaits the advent of the guitar-mounted compact disc player to cut down on expensive musicians, and the head-enveloping personal cinema with popcorn hopper. And there's no reason why you couldn't be the one to turn dreams into reality. Of course it would be unrealistic to suppose that every invention will find a ready market. You will have to be a little discriminating about your inventions. Ideas such as a three-wheeled, pedal-powered electric tricycle with handlebars under the rider's bottom are obviously too silly to bother your bank manager about, and trying to invent a thick-tyred bicycle with no mudguards that children can do acrobatics with is clearly too ridiculous for words.

Your Very Own Olympic Gold Medal

While a privileged few canter gracefully around the racetracks of the world like bipedal gazelles or throw themselves impossible distances into the air, the rest of the flabby-muscled, listless world spectates in mournful envy. Not just because of the unattainability of those taut frames and fluid limbs but also because of the glittering prizes that such attributes can achieve.

Winning a gold medal in a major sporting event is not simply confirmation that an athlete has reached a pinnacle of excellence, but a passport to international acclaim and significant material rewards. In short, once again someone is getting rich and famous and it's not you. How unfair it seems to so many of those gazing with glazed eyes at the television screen. How unfair that, were it not for a continuing excess of food and drink, long hours endured sitting motionless behind a desk and a fondness for the same once the working day is done, you too could be spraying everyone with champagne and shovelling money into the bank for rubbing yourself all over with a well-known deodorant.

After all, some of us have to keep the cogs of industry and commerce turning and cannot spend hours making sweat or waving huge pieces of metal about. The time has come to change all this. With a little bit of thought the many benefits of international stardom can be enjoyed even by those who spend most of their time on the beach sheltering from a veritable avalanche of kicked sand.

This doesn't mean that you will have to spend days in a steam oven rendering yourself down, or pounding across the countryside frightening motorists like a ground-effect Zeppelin and returning to a repast of chaff and granulated milk. It means applying yourself to some original thinking liberally sprinkled with deviousness. If you're not up to catapulting yourself through the sky on the end of a long bit of wood or hurtling round and round in circles showing your teeth

A real gold medal is 2 inches across, and has assay marks and 9ct (about 30mph) stamped on it. Don't be fobbed off with cheap imitations.

you must select a sport where the lack of serious competition may allow you to shine. If you're shrewd enough you may stumble upon an international event which nobody else has spotted.

Olympic Standard Hurling Hanky
(monogrammed class)

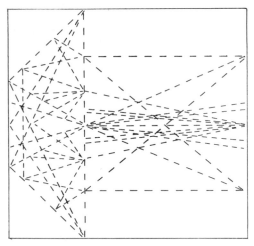

Simplified folding diagram

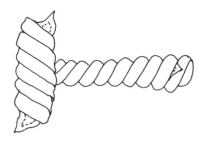

Hanky folded ready for hurling. (You won't
get this right first time).

Synchronized wrestling would be a good place to start as you need neither fitness nor strength to excel. An attractive costume and a small measure of lumbering grace is all that is required. Advance preparation should consist of building up the cheek muscles in order to maintain that glorious smile through headlock and flying mare. Practice blowing kisses to yourself in the mirror with a carrier bag full of housebricks suspended from each corner until your labial muscles positively ripple.

Hurling the handkerchief is a sport at which you may easily prove to be of world-beating status, particularly if you don't tell anyone else about it. If you set about it quietly enough your first throw could be a world record and if anyone challenges you, you could change the rules and sew stones in the hem. Then just sit back and wait for the sponsorship offers to come flooding in from linen and tissue manufacturers the whole world over.

Weed-flicking, in which small tufts of unwanted vegetation are launched over a medium height wooden fence into a neighbour's garden, falls into this class and if the event does attract opponents, make sure that your own garden is the venue and you will benefit whatever the result.

If these events are too energetic to appeal and you prefer something with more style and less brutish physical qualities why not turn your attention to Show Jumping and Dressage for Non-Riders. This is far more to the point than the usual equestrian events where certain imponderables such as the ability of the horse itself confuse the issue. There are material benefits to be gained from announcing yourself as Ron Apex Double Glazing before running under the first jump.

But these are all events less likely to attract the public eye than those which must take place in the midst of an athletic gathering, and some of you might yearn to participate in international events involving competitors of every kind. You will therefore need to devise sports in which you interact with some of the leading names in the sporting hall of fame.

The Ankle-Biting Hurdles could well be your event and will bring you into intimate contact with your heroes of the track. As soon as an important hurdling event has begun, rush out from the field and lurk under one of the hurdles, biting as many of the runners' ankles as you can before the umpires haul you off.

Swimming events too have many possibilities such as Backwards Swimming, Straddling the High Board Before Falling All Curled Up and Lying On the Bottom of the Pool Without Breathing for Ages. This general area also includes secondary events like Staying Under the Shower When it's Far Too Hot, and Stepping On Soap.

If you are hopeful of amassing great wealth through sport the cultivation of sponsors is all important. The ones to look for are those who cannot find a way of applying their product to the sporting scene. Sporting equipment and clothing manufacturers have all the conventional sports sewn up so there are hundreds of commercial concerns out there with money to burn and

Some newly introduced Olympic events. On the left, balancing lots of different things on top of each other. This is a timed event and ladders are not allowed (nor are stilts). On the right, Women's Low-level Formation Sky-diving in Period Costume. At the bottom, tense team-mates psyche themselves up for the timed Doll Shattering event. The studs and heel of the boots must be torn off bare-handed or dentally.

Eileen Carruthers was just another 100lb housewife and mother of two until she took up horse lifting. Now she's the Ladies' World Champion and an example to us all.

nothing to sponsor. You should therefore try and evolve a new sport taking this fact into account. I have no doubt that the Central Electricity Generating Board would invest substantial sums to have their name emblazoned on the back of the winner of The Human Catherine Wheel Relay. Not to be outdone, the Society of Hot Air Balloonists would invest heavily in the Bean Eater Marathon in the interest of sponsoring a new resource for their members.

But excelling at your game is often not enough to attract attention to your sponsor and behaviour on and off the field is extremely important. You simply must learn not to control your temper and to get absolutely furious whenever possible. The weather, the lady in the pink fluffy hat in the crowd, a tuft of grass, all should drive you into a financially advantageous frenzy at every televised meeting (see *Be a Megastar*).

Once you have attained international renown in your sport you must be prepared for the stresses of stardom that come with success. You will experience acute loneliness over long distances and your exclusive involvement with an artificial, solitary environment will subject you to many temptations. If you can resist the hazards of steroid abuse and liniment addiction, which can turn a healthy athlete into a solid mound of pungent meat in no time, you will remain on the Gold Medal Trail for days at a time.

YES, YES YOU, COULD BE A ROCK

MEGASTAR

While others are rushing about shouting at each other on the floor of the Stock Exchange or labouring over piles of complicated paperwork late into the night in order to make their first million, a few bright sparks have found the easy way to unimaginable wealth. By becoming an international rock megastar you could save years of toil and stress and be adored at the same time.

The first thing you must do is to decide exactly what sort of megastar you wish to be, and this will depend to some degree on your musical ability. If you are one of the lucky ones who have absolutely none at all, the world is your oyster because you will be spared the torment of wondering whether or not you are compromising your artistic integrity. Provided you are prepared to choose Heavy Metal as your genre you are all set to rocket to megastardom.

The secret of heavy metal music is to find a level of volume that everyone who likes real music hates and everyone who hates real music loves. This means making it as loud as technology permits, but for the novice megastar the equipment needed to bill yourself as the loudest rock band in the world is very expensive.

Megasound

A perfect solution can be found in any good military surplus scrap dealer's yard. Purchase three good Rolls Royce RB211 engines from a retired 747 and mount them on the front of the stage. This will also avoid the need for expensive guitars as even a cheap Spanish instrument provides enough volume when sucked through the engines and broadcast to the audience at 42,000lb of thrust. At this level of sound amplification you do not need to be able to play a single note in tune for maximum head-banging effect to be achieved.

Vocals can be amplified in the same way because the lyrics don't need to be intelligible for heavy metal fans. In any case most songs consist of wailing, shrieking and primeval grunting in time with the output of the obligatory enraged drummer.

above
Even if you look like this, with a bit of grooming and surgery megastardom could be yours.

If you want to keep your day job you can wear a mask to wow the fans by night. But try to show a bit more enthusiasm in your publicity photographs.

None of the performers ought to stand too close to the intakes of your amplification equipment. A gimmick is one thing but spraying yourselves over the entire concert hall as a fine red mist, though undoubtedly spec- tacularly original, will not help your career in the long run.

Finding an image for your heavy metal band consists of appearing more sinister than anyone else. Black leather every- thing is obligatory, preferably with thousands of little chrome studs for maximum menace, and all members of the ensemble should glue the contents of horsehair cushions to their exposed torsos. A gaunt, haunted appearance can be achieved by removing all the skin from your head. This can be thrown to the enraptured audience as a memento of the show.

Movement is an integral part of rock and roll and a handy tip is to replace the stage boarding with a giant trampoline so that the performers can really move about. A safety net suspended above the stage will ensure that artistes descend in time for the next number.

Bad Behaviour

Your rock image must be maintained both on stage and off, and this will mean familiarizing yourself with some standard rock star ploys. Whenever you check into a new hotel, YMCA or campsite, unpack your things carefully and go completely berserk. Throw the complimentary soap on to the floor and stamp on it, block up the toilet with a pillow, set fire to the wastepaper basket and be sick under the bed. If you're not really

famous yet, only do this in someone else's room.

The same technique can be used in restaurants, clubs or motorway service areas and is an important part of media interviews. In the latter instance further refinements can be added such as dribbling while you talk, poking food or cigarettes up your nose and biting off the top of the microphone. When dealing with media folk always grunt clearly and concisely and sprinkle your monologue with a few big words that you totally misunderstand in order to make the reporter feel that he has either gone completely mad or is totally out of touch with street jargon.

If you are allergic to leather and bourbon, Punk Rock is quite a good alternative. The rules are essentially the same except everyone plays saxophones, wears dustbin liners and sticks skewers through parts of their heads. Vocal styles differ too. Instead of screaming and growl-

Yes you do need a stage image but this one isn't really working. We suggest that these two should wear fishnet tights instead of trousers.

This illustration shows how easily you can totally transform your image by means of just clothing and decoration.

The right image for the right music. Top row from left: Glitter Rock (happy little songs). New Wave/Gay Rock (sad little songs). New Romantics (really boring songs). Reggae (incomprehensible songs). The Blues (complicated songs ending in 'baby'). Marching songs, protest songs and crooning are all unfashionable so being a hit with any of them is going to be an uphill job.

ing, the singer recites things like the telephone directory or the communist manifesto as monotonously as possible.

If you feel that these musical forms lack sufficient sophistication there are plenty of options such as **Glitter Rock** where you sing happy little songs disguised as Barbara Cartland, or **New Wave/Gay Rock** where you sing sad little songs disguised as Barbara Cartland, or **The New Romantics** where you sing really boring songs disguised as an undertaker.

As a **Reggae** artist you sing incomprehensible songs disguised as someone who has fallen head first into a huge bowl of wholemeal spaghetti. Another ethnic possibility is to sing the **Blues.** This is more complicated as you need to think of at least three different phrases for each song which are then sung in various sequences ending with 'Babeee'. Gargle with sand every night to get the right vocal quality, and give your tailor completely the wrong measurements when the time comes to order your shiny stage suit.

Whatever style of music you choose to adopt there are certain important rules to follow if you are to achieve megastardom. Always be late for concerts and don't show up at all for the really important ones. Even if you are just going down to the hotel bar for a quick drink, tear your clothes and blame it on hit-and-run fans. To save money you could have all the seams joined with Velcro.

Once you are a megastar you must purchase a vast and isolated mansion and sever all connections with the outside world. Timing is very important here as if you make this move before you actually are a megastar, there is a good chance you will starve to death before anyone misses you.

Which brings us to another aspect of your career as a megastar. Retirement is only the beginning and provides the opportunity for either The Comeback or Posthumous Megastardom. In the former instance you must pay someone to drag you kicking and screaming back into the limelight so that you can perform once more the inimitable songs that drove you into obscurity in the first place. In the latter instance you will have to trust your beneficiaries to handle everything on your behalf.

Appendix

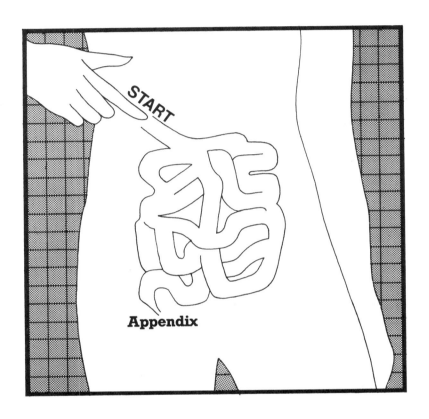

START

Appendix